Shush-Hush Quiet Activities

by Nancy Bosse

Activity 1	On the Road Again	2
Activity 2	Hurry Up and Wait!	4
Activity 3	It Takes Two	6
Activity 4	The More the Merrier	8
Activity 5	Oodles of Doodles	10
Activity 6	The Wonderful World of Words	12
Activity 7	Number Sense? Don't Count On It!	14
Activity 8	A Code You Can Count On	15
Activity 9	Fast Finger Fortune Flicker	16
Activity 10	Jumping Frog	19
Activity 11	Q Is for Quiet and Quilts	20
Activity 12	Creative Creatures	21
Activity 13	Going Nuts!	22
Activity 14	Be a Pinball Wizard!	23
Activity 15	Let Your Fingers Do the Talking	24
Activity 16	Hands Down!	26
Activity 17	Dynamic Dotted Duels	27
Activity 18	All in a Row?	30
Activity 19	Toothpick Wonders	32
Activity 20	Battle Brigade	34
Activity 21	Penny for Your Thoughts	36
Activity 22	It's in the Cards	38
Activity 23	Domino Delight	41
Activity 24	Tantalizing Tangrams	44
	Solutions	47

Editorial: Kim Carlson, Kristy Kugler, Paul Rawlins
Art and Design: Andy Carlson, Robyn Funk, Magen Mitchell, Amanda Sorensen

© 2006, Rainbow Bridge Publishing, Greensboro, North Carolina 27425. The purchase of this material entitles the buyer to reproduce worksheets and activities for classroom use only—not for commercial resale. Reproduction of these materials for an entire school or district is prohibited. No part of this book may be reproduced (except as noted above), stored in a retrieval system, or transmitted in any form or by any means (mechanically, electronically, recording, etc.) without the prior written consent of Carson-Dellosa Publishing Co., Inc.

Printed in the USA • All rights reserved.   ISBN 1-59441-721-0

Activity 1

On the Road Again

Sometimes it feels like we spend more time in our cars than in our homes. Whether you're riding to soccer practice, to piano lessons, or on a cross-country excursion, these games will help pass the time and keep you and your parents sane!

Peace and Quiet

Here's a great game! No one can speak until someone spots a certain object. Some things to look for might be a license plate with the letter Q on it, a sign for a certain gas station or food stop, a black dog, or a man with a hat. The person who spots the object first can choose the next thing to look for.

Color Cars

Have each player choose a car color. Each time a player sees a car that is her color, that player gets one point. First one to 20 is the winner.

Signs

Players have to find each letter of the alphabet in order from the signs along the road. You may only use one letter from each sign.

Map It!

Print out a map or directions from your home to where you're going. You can find these at www.mapquest.com or www.RandMcnally.com. Keep track of where you've been and how much farther you have to go.

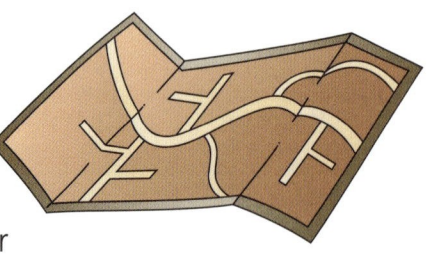

Explore 24: Shush-Hush Quiet Activities

Explore 24: Shush-Hush Quiet Activities   Page 3

On the Road Again

Wacky Phrases

Spot a license plate and write down the letters on it. Use the letters in the order they appear on the license plate as the first letter of each word in a phrase. For example, MKR could be Most Kids Rock! Try to think of as many phrases as you can. When you've run out of ideas, look for another license plate.

It All Adds Up

Write down the numbers from a license plate and add them up. When you have the answer, look for another set of numbers.

Number Game

Find the digits 0 through 9 in order on license plates. Then find double numbers beginning with 00 through 99. For a real challenge, try to find triples.

Activity 2

Hurry Up and Wait!

Next time you are stuck at the doctor's office or in some other waiting room, try some of these games to pass the time.

What's in a Name?

Make as many words as you can with the letters in the title of a magazine. For example, from the title *Ranger Rick* you can make the words *anger, rang, Nick, ran, can, rack,* and *gear.* Play alone, or challenge someone waiting with you. The person who makes the most words wins.

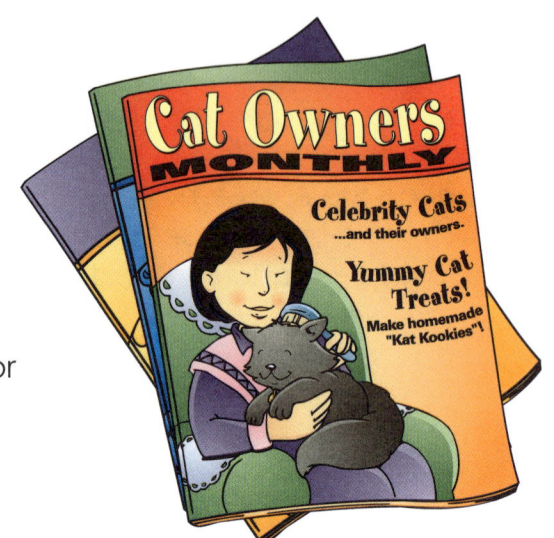

Alphabet Search

Here's another game you can play by yourself or with someone else. Open a magazine to any page. Look for the letter *a*, then *b*, and so on. If the next letter in the alphabet is not found on that page, turn the page and keep looking. Continue until you've found all the letters of the alphabet. If you're playing with someone else, take turns finding the letters.

Alphabetical Objects

Look around the room and find something that begins with the letter *a*. Maybe you'll see an aquarium or an air conditioner. Keep going through the alphabet. When you get to some of the harder letters like *j, q, x, y,* and *z*, be creative! Find items that have the letter in them, like a bo*x* of tissues for *x*.

Explore 24: Shush-Hush Quiet Activities

Explore 24: Shush-Hush Quiet Activities

Hurry Up and Wait!

Magazine Spotto

Challenge your parent or a sibling to a friendly game of Magazine Spotto! Together, make up a list of items to find, or use the one below. Then each player chooses a magazine. At the signal, each player scours the magazine for the first item on the list. The first person to find the item scores one point. The person with the most points at the end of the list wins! Create your own lists.

Can you spot a...
- dog
- toothbrush
- car advertisement
- smiling child
- glass of milk
- girl in pigtails
- dessert
- straw
- baby
- bicycle
- cow
- flower
- computer
- watch
- book

Activity 2

Activity 3

It Takes Two

Here are some quiet games to play when you've got someone to be quiet with you.

Back Me Up

Have your friend close his eyes and sit with his back to you. Write on your friend's back with your finger. Challenge your friend to guess what you've written. Then trade places. Start with letters, and then try writing words or secret messages.

The Never-Ending Sentence

Create a crazy sentence. One player begins by saying the first word of a sentence. The next player says another word. The player that finishes the sentence wins. A word cannot be used in the same sentence more than once.

I'm Thinking of a Number

Think of a number between 1 and 100. Challenge your partner to guess the number by asking questions that can be answered "yes" or "no." Your partner could ask questions like "Is your number more than 50?" "Is your number an odd number?" or "Can your number be divided by 3?"

Explore 24: Shush-Hush Quiet Activities

Explore 24: Shush-Hush Quiet Activities

It Takes Two

This ancient game can be played indoors or outdoors. If you're outdoors, you can play this game by scooping out little holes in the ground. If you're indoors, use small containers like paper cups or paper bowls. Set your cups as shown below.

Mancala

Each player sits on one side of the rows of cups. Put three tokens (pennies, pebbles, or beans) in each cup except the two on the ends. Players "own" the end cup on their right and the cups in front of them. The object of the game is to collect the most tokens in your end cup.

To play, the first player scoops up all the tokens from one of his cups. Then he drops one token in each cup beginning with the first cup to the right. If the player has enough tokens, he puts one in his end cup. Tokens that are put in the end cup remain in the end cup. If the player has more tokens after dropping one in his end cup, he keeps dropping tokens in each cup going around the rows counterclockwise. The player does not drop a token into his opponent's end cup. If the last piece a player drops lands in an empty cup on his row, he can move that token and all the tokens from the cup across from it into his end cup.

Players take turns until one player has no more tokens in his cups. Then the game is over. The player with the most tokens in his or her end space wins. (You can find more Mancala rules in books or on the Internet.)

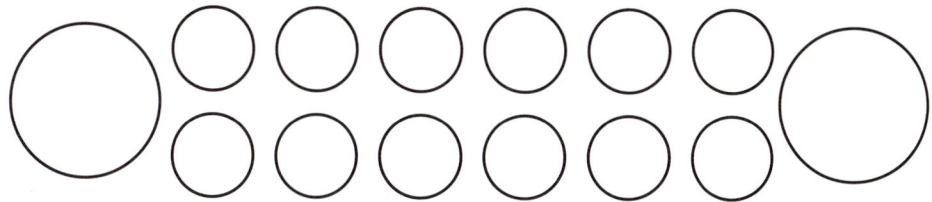

Activity 4

The More the Merrier

More may be merrier, but it's sure to be louder, too! Here are a few games to play when your group needs to stay quiet.

Ghost

The first player says a letter. The next person thinks of a word that begins with that letter and adds the next letter. Players each add a letter until they can no longer add a letter or until they form a complete word. For example the first person says, "b." The next person cannot say "e" because "be" is a word. The second person could say "b-o," thinking of the word "bought." The third person thinks of a word that starts with "b-o" and adds a letter. Let's say the third person adds "c," but the fourth person cannot think of a word that starts "b-o-c." The fourth person is out. The game continues until only one person is left.

If a person can't think of a letter to add and suspects that the player before didn't have a real word in mind, that person can challenge the previous player. The challenged player has a chance to say the word he was thinking of. If the player was bluffing and didn't have a specific word in mind, that player is out instead of the person who challenged.

Telephone

Have everyone sit in a circle. The first player makes up a short sentence or phrase and whispers it to the player on the right. Everyone must listen closely because the phrase can't be repeated. The second player whispers the sentence to the next person and so on until the message comes back to the player to the left of the first person. The last person in the circle says the sentence out loud. Then the first person says what the original sentence was. How different was the message after it went all the way around the circle?

Explore 24: Shush-Hush Quiet Activities

The More the Merrier

Murder

You need a small piece of paper for each player. Put an X on one piece of paper. Leave the rest of the papers blank. Fold all the papers and put them in a bag. Have all the players sit in a circle. Pass the bag around and have everyone pick a piece of paper without showing it to anyone else. The person with the X is the murderer. Once everyone has a piece of paper, the game begins. The murderer begins by secretly winking at people. When a person sees the murderer wink at her, she is dead and quietly puts her head down. The murderer continues to wink at people until someone catches him in the act. A person who is winked at cannot reveal the murderer. Only someone who sees the murderer wink at someone else can call out, "I know the murderer." If the player is incorrect, she is out of the game. If the player guesses correctly, that player wins the game.

Take Note!

You need a deck of cards and at least three players for this game. The object of the game is to get four of the same card (4 tens, for example) or to notice when someone else does. One player shuffles the deck and deals four cards to each player. The remaining cards are placed in a pile to the dealer's right. All players look at their cards and choose one to discard. The dealer draws a card from the pile and decides which of his five cards he will pass on. At the signal, all the players pass their discarded card face down to the left. Players look at their new card. The dealer discards one card, draws another, and play continues. When someone gets four of the same card, that player quietly puts her cards on the table while continuing to pass and receive cards. As players see that someone has laid her cards down, they do the same, even if they don't have four matching cards. The last person to put her hand down loses that round.

Activity 4

Activity 5

Oodles of Doodles

Drawing is always a fun way to pass the time when you need to be quiet.

Symmetry Portraits

Do you know what **symmetry** is? Symmetry is when both sides of something are exactly the same. Find a full-page symmetrical picture in a magazine. People and animal faces work best, but any picture that is symmetrical will work. Carefully cut the page out of the magazine. Next, cut the picture in half. Glue one-half of the picture on a piece of paper. Now draw the other half of the picture. You'll be amazed at how well you do!

Doodle Dee Doos

Ask your parent or a friend to make a large squiggle on a blank piece of paper. Turn the squiggle into a picture of something.

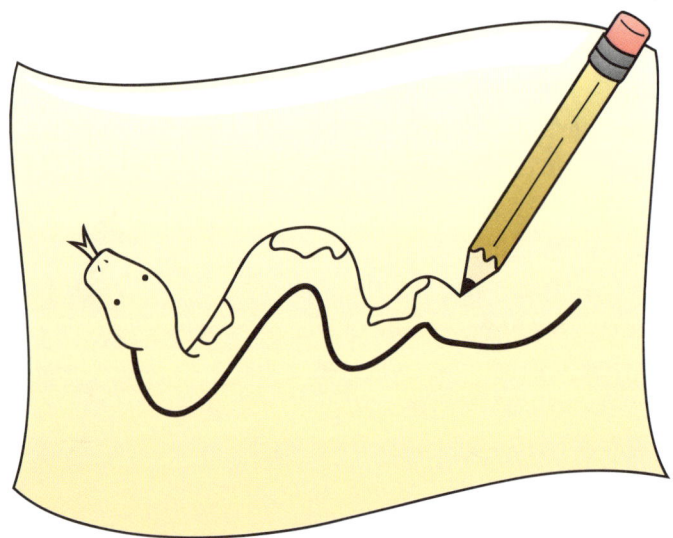

Explore 24: Shush-Hush Quiet Activities

Page 11

Oodles of Doodles

Thumbprint Art

Do you feel like you're all thumbs when it comes to art? Well, for this type of art, that's perfect! All you need are those thumbs of yours, an ink pad, and some felt-tip markers. Check out the examples on this page. Then let your imagination be your guide. For more ideas, check out Ed Emberley's books on thumbprint art.

Doodle Thinking

Try to draw these shapes without taking your pencil off the paper. (The answers are on page 47.)

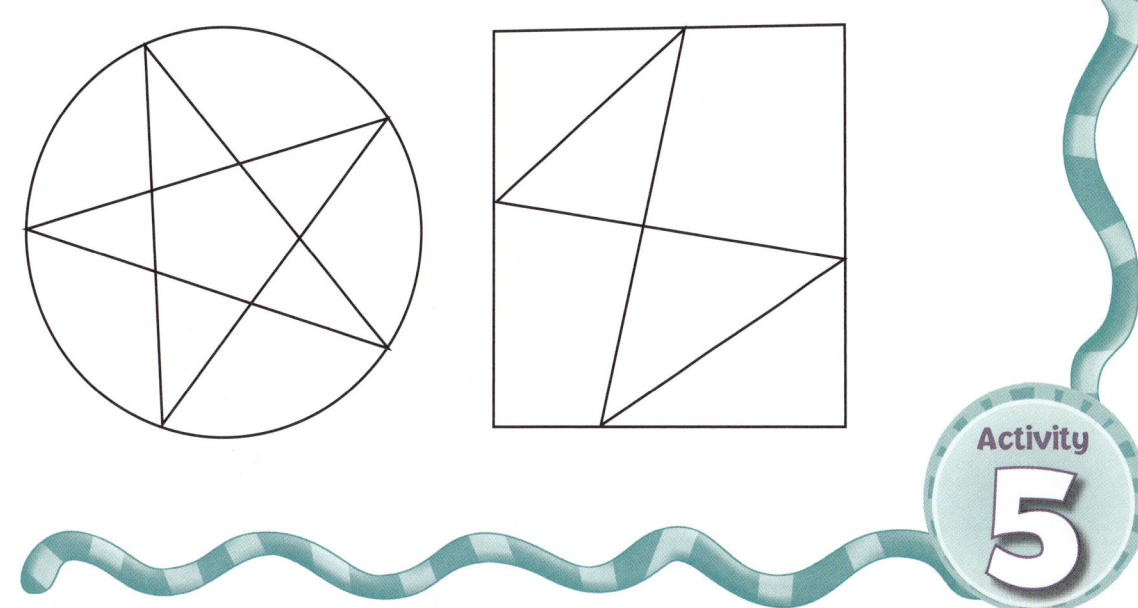

Activity 5

Activity 6

The Wonderful World of Words

Challenge a friend to some of these word games when you have to be quiet.

Hangman

Begin by drawing a gallows as shown.

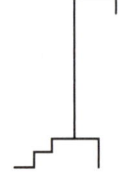

Think of a word and draw one blank space underneath the gallows for each letter in the word. Have a friend try to guess your word by guessing letters that may be in the word. If your friend guesses a letter in the word, put the letter in the correct space or spaces. If the letter is not in the word, draw a head coming down from the gallows. Add a body part for each wrong letter. If the word is guessed before the person on the gallows is complete, the guesser wins.

For a harder game, use phrases and titles instead

of just a word. To make the game easier, add more parts to the hangman, such as hands and feet or eyes and a mouth.

Categories

Each player draws a 5 x 5 grid on a piece of paper. Decide on four categories, such as names, animals, foods, and flowers. Write the categories in four boxes across the top of the grid. Then choose four letters to go down the first column. Everyone uses the same letters. When someone says "Go," everyone tries to think of words that begin with the letter in the left column and fit under the category in the top row. After five minutes, read the words. Each original word is worth two points, and each word that matches someone else's word is worth one point.

	Animal	Fruit	Color	Flower
W				
E				
K				
T				

For a harder game, use more categories and more letters.

Explore 24: Shush-Hush Quiet Activities

The Wonderful World of Words

Mystery Word

The object of the game is to discover the mystery word. The first player writes a word at the top of a piece of paper and then folds the paper to hide the word. Then that player draws two columns. In each column, the player makes a dash for each letter in the mystery word.

The second player guesses a word and writes it on the dashes in column 1. If a letter from that word is in the same spot as that letter in the mystery word, the first player writes the letter in the correct spot in column 2. If the player guesses a correct letter but it is not in the right location, it is written in column 2 with a ring around it. Play continues until the mystery word is guessed.

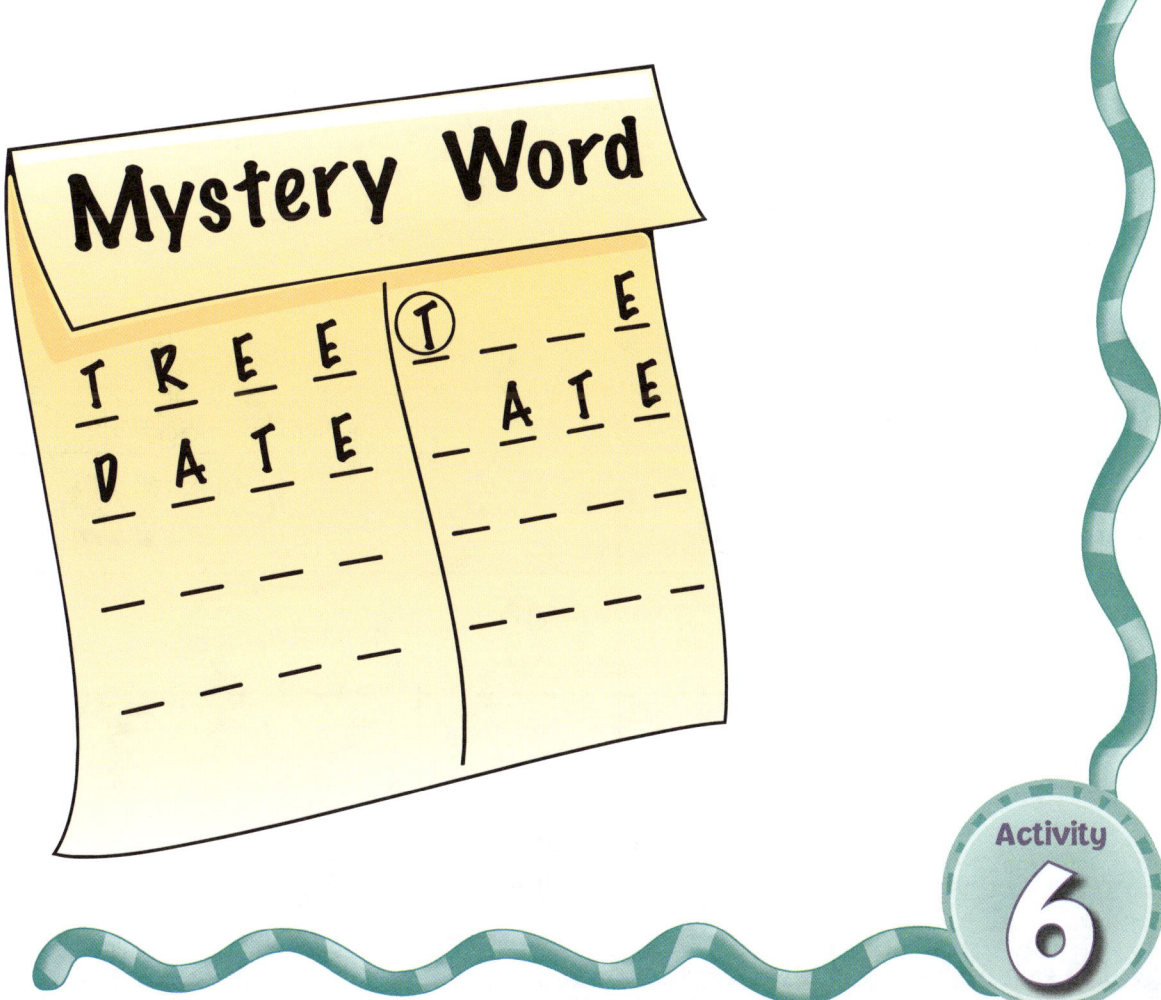

Activity 7

Number Sense? Don't Count on It!

Here are some quiet number games and tricks that will amaze your parents and friends. You might even amaze yourself!

Equal Numbers

Look at the circles. If you move one number from one of the circles into another circle, the sum of all the numbers in each circle will be equal. You'll find the solution on page 47.

It All Adds Up

Use the numbers 0 through 9 in the boxes so that each column and each row adds up to 20. See the solution on page 47.

5			12
	0		
			1
	13	4	

Explore 24: Shush-Hush Quiet Activities   Page 14

Explore 24: Shush-Hush Quiet Activities

Page 15

A Code You Can Count On

Here's a secret code that you can use to write notes to your friends. Can you make up your own secret code?

Try to figure out the message below. You'll find the solution on page 47. Try writing a message of your own.

A	B	C	D	E	F	G	H	I	J	K	L	M	N	O	P	Q	R	S	T	U	V	W	X	Y	Z
1	2	3	4	5	6	7	8	9	10	11	12	13	14	15	16	17	18	19	20	21	22	23	24	25	26

__ __ __ __ __ __ __   __ __
19 9 12 5 14 3 5   9 19

__ __ __ __ __ __
7 15 12 4 5 14

Use the chart below to create your own code by shifting the letters one, two, or three places. For example, A = D, F = I, and Z = C.

A	B	C	D	E	F	G	H	I	J	K	L	M	N	O	P	Q	R	S	T	U	V	W	X	Y	Z

Activity 8

Activity 9

Fast Finger Fortune Flicker

Whew! Try saying that ten times fast! You'll have as much fun making this flicker as you will playing with it when you're done!

Directions:

1. Cut around the outside edges of the Fortune Flicker found on page 17. Flip the Flicker to the blank side. Fold the four corners to the middle.

2. Flip the Flicker back to the front and fold the four corners to the middle on this side.

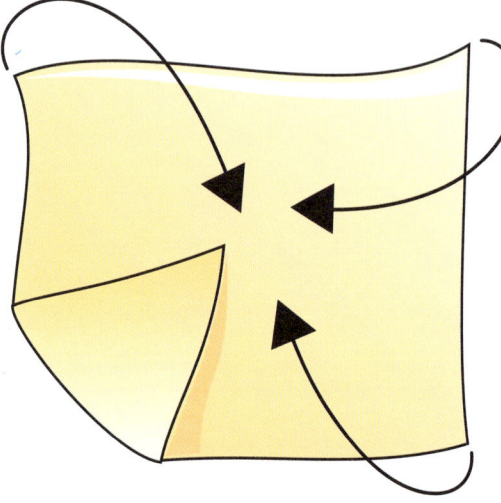

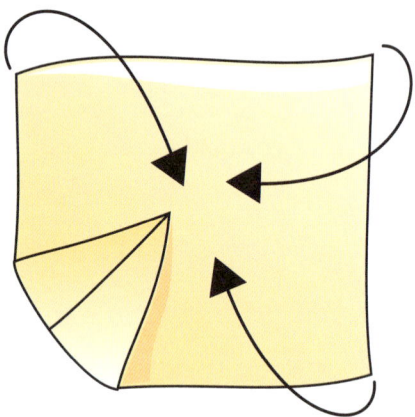

3. Now fold the Flicker in half toward the middle to make a rectangle. Slip your thumbs and index fingers under the four corner flaps.

4. Open and close the Flicker by opening and closing your thumbs and fingers, first one way and then the other. You can also use one hand to play with your Flicker. To use one hand, put all your fingers except for your pinkie under the four corner flaps and open and close your thumbs and fingers to open and close the Flicker.

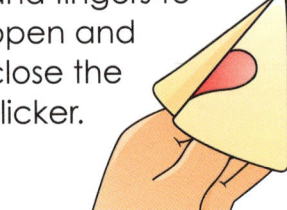

Explore 24: Shush-Hush Quiet Activities   Page 16

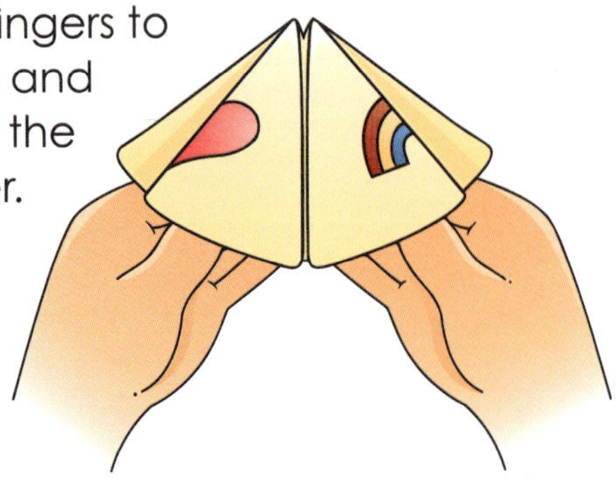

How to Tell Fortunes

Put your fingers in the Flicker. Have your friend ask a yes or no question. Then ask him to choose one of the four pictures. Spell out the name of the picture, opening and closing the Flicker in opposite directions each time you say a letter. Hold the Flicker open and ask the friend to choose one of the four numbers. Again, open and close the Flicker in opposite directions according to the number chosen. Then ask your friend to pick another number from the four showing. Open the flap and read the answer to your friend's question.

Activity 9

Explore 24: Shush-Hush Quiet Activities

Jumping Frog

Jumping Jiminy, this frog is fun to make and to play with, too! And, best of all, it's quiet.

Start with an 8 ½" x 5 ½" piece of paper. After you get the hang of making frogs, you may want to experiment with smaller paper. The smaller frogs seem to jump better. To make the frog jump, push down on its lower back. Challenge your friends to frog jumping contests.

Follow these steps:

1. Make 3 folds. First, fold the top left corner to the right edge of the paper. Unfold, then fold the top right corner to the left edge of the paper. Unfold again and fold the top edge toward the bottom edge of the paper, with the fold line creasing in the middle of the X created by the first two folds.

2. Unfold the paper, then fold the middle crease in on both sides, bringing the top corners toward the bottom.

3. Fold the two pointed corners up to the top point.

4. Fold the two straight sides to the middle.

5. Fold the bottom edge up to the crease. Then fold that edge back down to form the legs.

6. Decorate your new little friend!

Activity 10

Activity 11

Q is for Quiet and Quilts!

Making beautiful quilts is an art and a craft.

Cut colored construction paper into 1" squares. Then cut some of the squares in half to form triangles. Experiment with the shapes to create pretty designs and patterns. Try different color and design combinations. When you've found a combination you like, glue the shapes in place on a piece of paper.

Explore 24: Shush-Hush Quiet Activities

Page 20

Creative Creatures

Here are some creatures you won't find in your backyard or at the zoo! See how many you can make.

Fold at least three 8 ½" x 11" pieces of paper in half lengthwise. Staple along the fold.

Leave the top and the bottom sheet whole. These will form the cover of your book. Cut the inside pages into thirds. On each page put marks at the cuts 1" and 2" from the bottom.

Draw a head on the first panel, a body on the second panel, and a tail on the third panel. Create a different creature on each page. Always be sure to connect the parts at the marks.

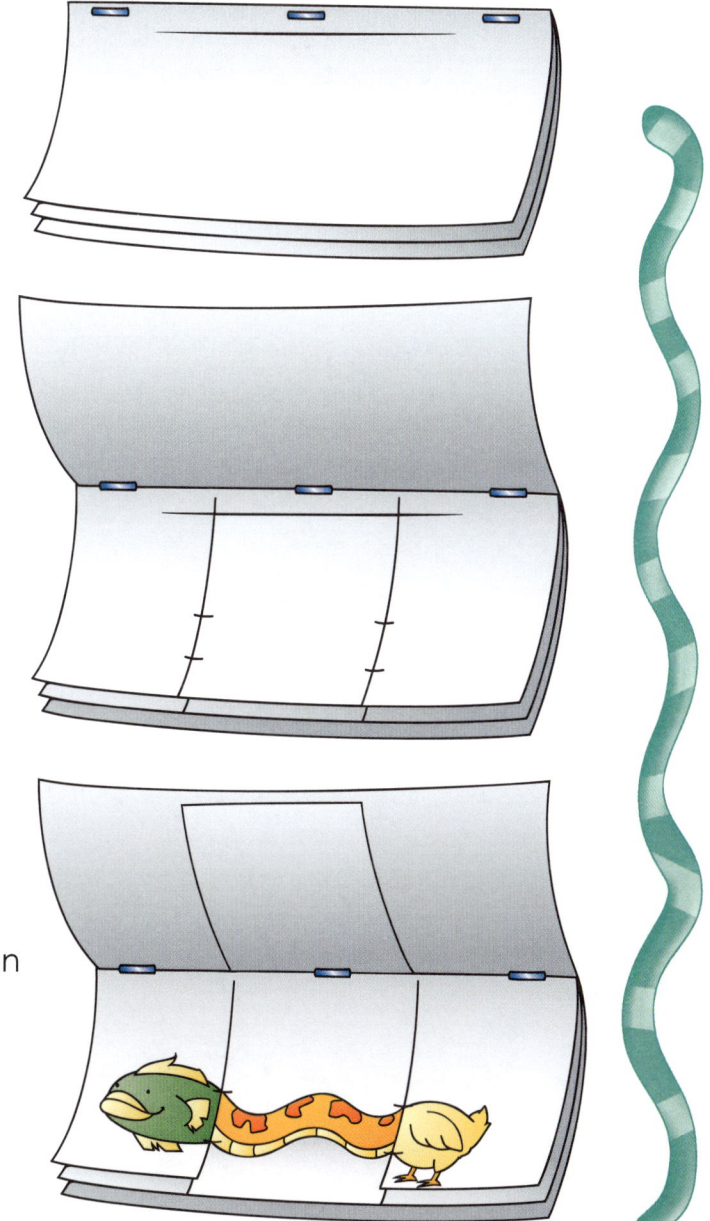

When you are finished, move the flaps to create different animals.

Activity 12

Activity 13

Going Nuts!

If the noise in your house is making your mother nuts, ask her for some walnuts in exchange for some peace and quiet.

You'll need an adult to help with this first step.
Crack several whole walnuts in half and clean out the meat. One way to crack them is to slide a screwdriver down the seam of the walnut. Be careful not to crack the half-shells when you do it.

Paint the walnut halves with poster paint. Use craft supplies like yarn, felt, and googly eyes to turn your walnut into a cute little critter.

When your walnut buddy is dry, you can put a marble under the shell and have races with your other walnut buddies. Or you can glue a piece of felt to the bottom, add a piece of magnetic tape to the bottom, and use it as a refrigerator magnet.

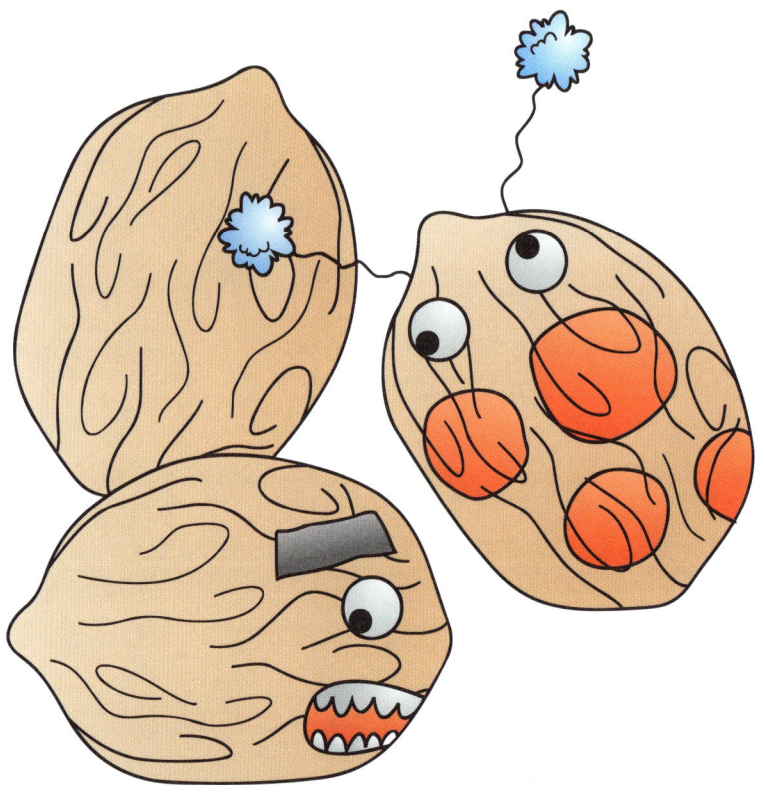

Explore 24: Shush-Hush Quiet Activities

Be a Pinball Wizard!

Here's a fun arcade-like game that you can make with a board, a hammer and nails, some rubber bands, a pencil, and a felt-tipped marker. Make sure to have an adult around to help you with this activity. Hammers and nails can be dangerous if you're not extra careful.

With a pencil, sketch your pinball board design. You'll probably want to have two starting points and at least three ways you can finish. Sketch a maze-like path from start to finish. Hammer nails along the path. Don't let the nails break through the wood! Stretch rubber bands between the nails to make several paths. Label your starting points and your finishing points. Give each finishing point different point values. Then start a marble at one of your starting points and let it roll.

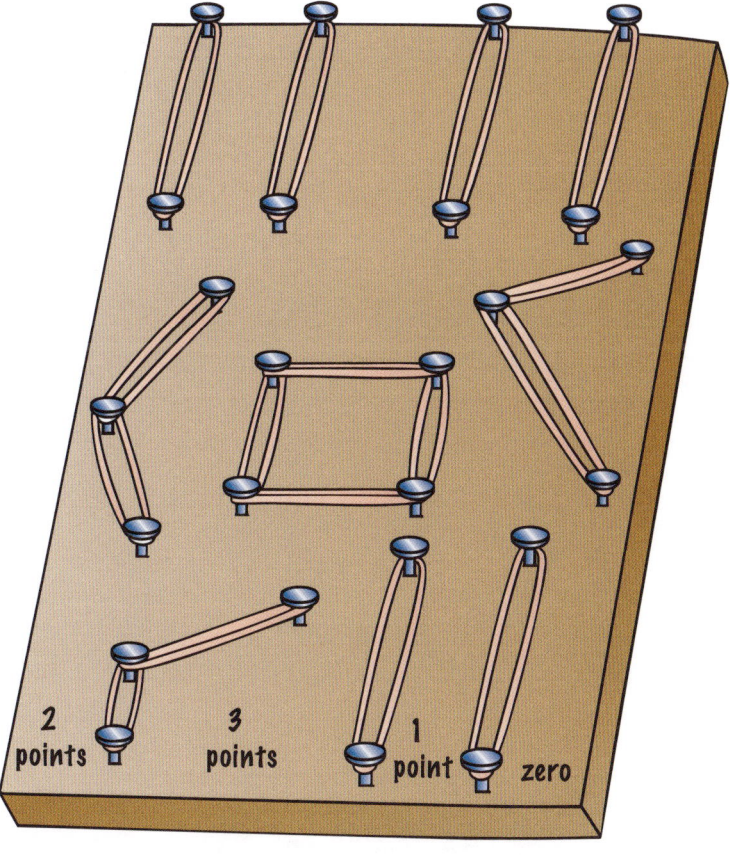

Activity 15

Let Your Fingers Do the Talking

(They are so much quieter!)
When it's time to be quiet and you still have things to say, let your fingers do the talking! Even the librarian can't object to finger spelling.

Use the chart on the next page to learn to spell words using the American Sign Language Alphabet. Then finger spell secret messages to your friends.

Use the chart on the next page to figure out the message below. You'll find the solution on page 48.

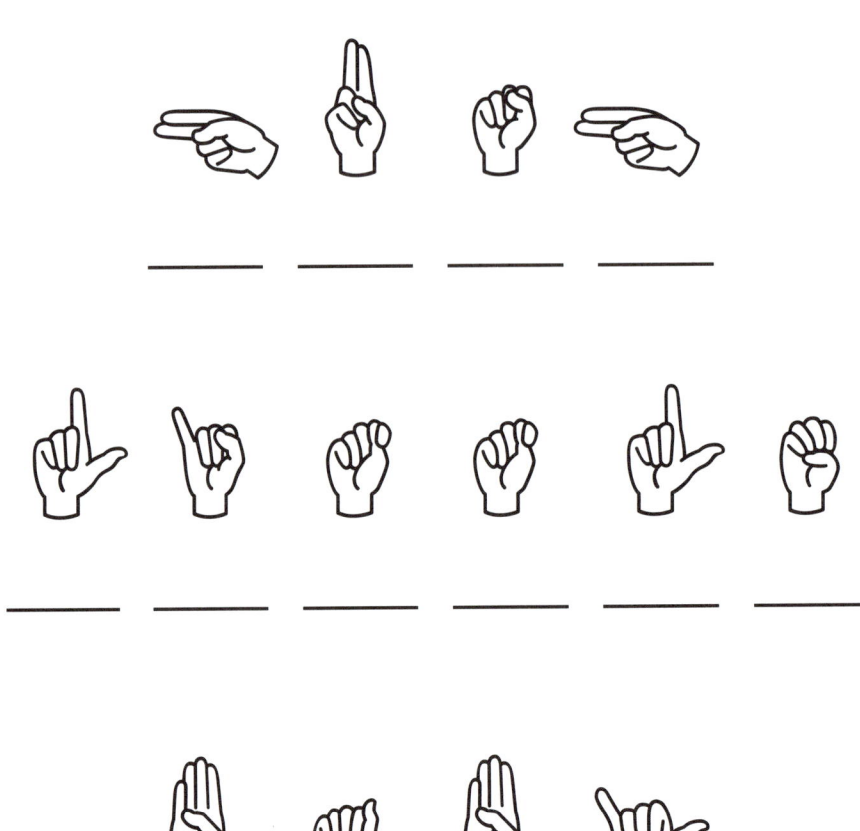

Explore 24: Shush-Hush Quiet Activities

American Sign Language Alphabet

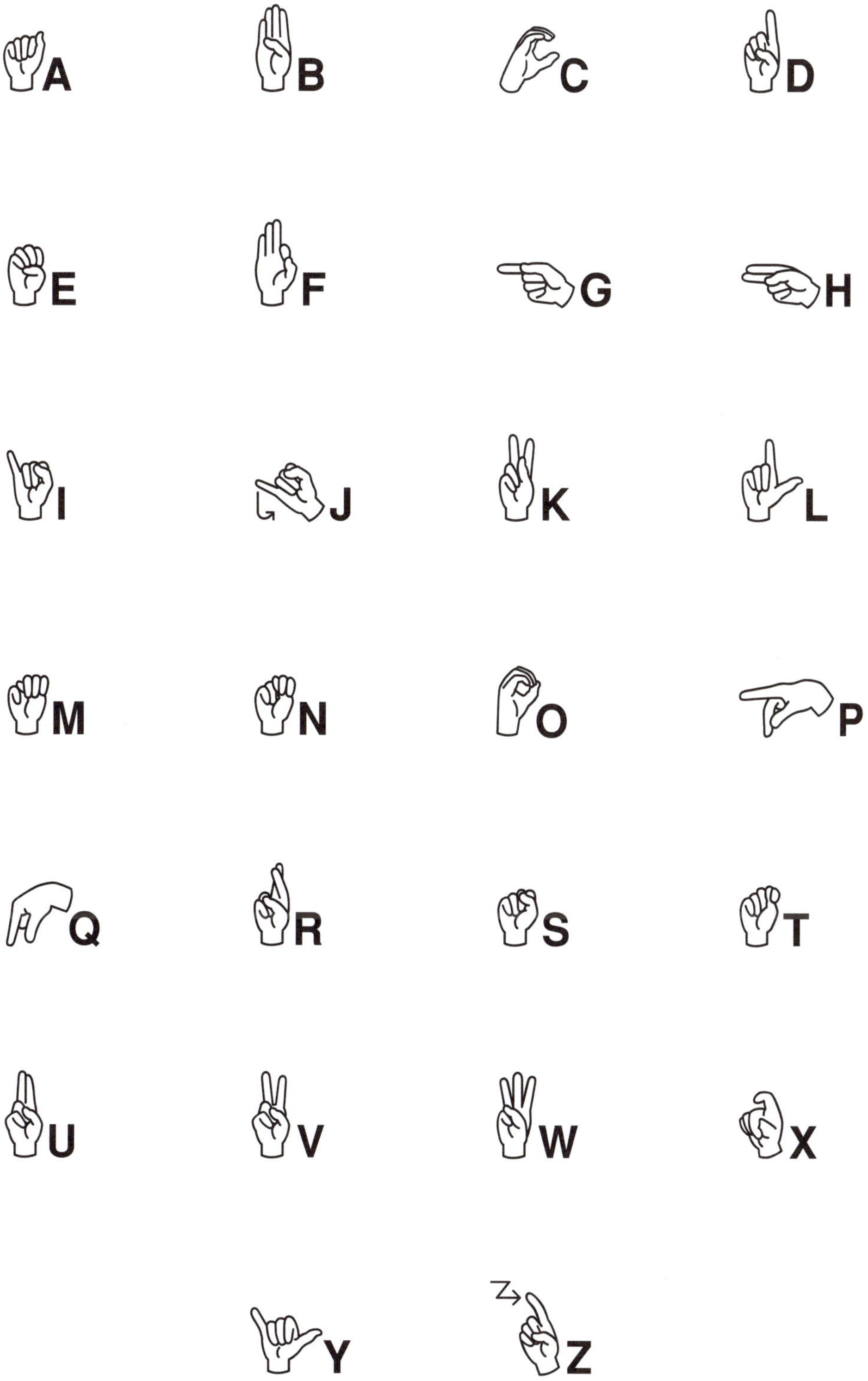
A
B
C
D
E
F
G
H
I
J
K
L
M
N
O
P
Q
R
S
T
U
V
W
X
Y
Z

Activity 15

Activity 16

Hands Down!

You'll always have the supplies on "hand" for these quiet games.

Rock, Paper, Scissors

Here is a game that needs no special equipment or set up. To play, players gently pound their fists into the palm of their hands, saying "One, two, three." On the count of three, each player shows rock, paper, or scissors (see illustration). Rock breaks scissors. Scissors cut paper. Paper covers rock. The winner scores one point. Continue until someone has 20 points.

Thumb Wrestling

Link the fingers of your right hand with the fingers of the right hand of your opponent. To begin a match, both players chant, "One, two, three, four, I declare a thumb war" as they cross their thumbs back and forth on their opponent's fist. The first person to pin the other player's thumb to his fist wins that round.

Flashing Finger Facts

You can play this with two to four players. Each player shakes her closed fist three times. On the third shake, each player flashes a number of fingers (0 to 5). The first person to say the correct total of fingers flashed wins. For example, if two people are playing this game, and one person flashes two fingers and the other person flashes one finger, the first person to say "three!" wins that game.

Explore 24: Shush-Hush Quiet Activities   Page 26

Explore 24: Shush-Hush Quiet Activities

Dynamic Dotted Duels

You'll go dotty over these games! All you need are a friend, a piece of paper, and a pencil or two.

Dots and Squares

Draw a large grid of dots. Players take turns drawing one line between two dots that are next to each other. Lines may *not* go diagonally. When a player draws a line that completes a square, she writes her initials inside the square. When all the squares have been completed, players count the number of squares with their initials. The player with the most squares wins.

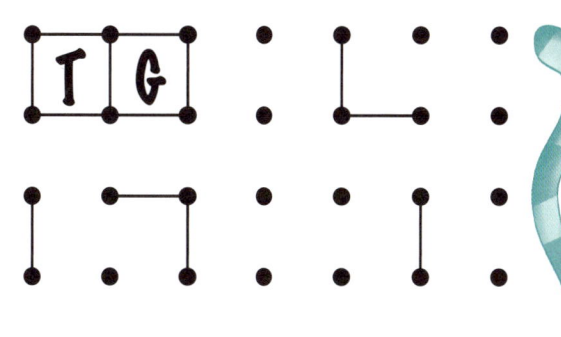

Dots and Triangles

This game is a lot like Dots and Squares. The biggest difference is the playing grid. Instead of a square grid, you'll be creating a pyramid. Make your pyramid with one dot on the top row, two dots on the second row, three dots on the third row, and so on. Players take turns drawing lines between dots to make triangles. In this game, of course, diagonal lines are allowed. When a player makes a triangle, he writes his initials in the triangle. The player with initials in the most triangles after all the dots have been connected wins.

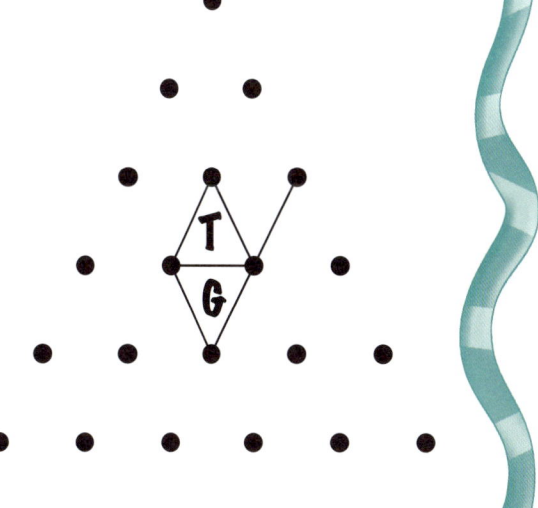

Activity 17

Activity 17

Dynamic Dotted Duels

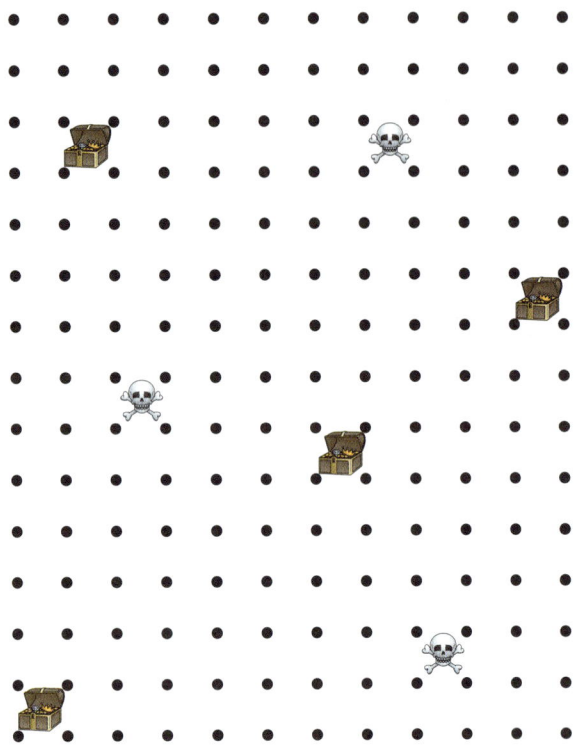

Dots and Treasures

This game is another twist on the Dots and Squares game. The rules are the same as the rules for Dots and Squares. However, this time you get bonus points for completing the squares around the treasure chests. Beware, though! You lose two points if you complete the square around a skull and crossbones. Play this game with a friend.

And Another Dots Game

In this game, you use a grid of dots like you do for Dots and Squares. The first player draws a line between two dots that are next to each other (no diagonal lines). The next player must draw a line going in the opposite direction between two dots. This means that one player will draw only horizontal lines, and the other player will draw only vertical lines. (Horizontal lines go across. Vertical lines go up and down.) Unlike Dots and Squares, in this game, no two lines may share a dot. Play continues until one of the players cannot form a line without connecting to a previously used dot. The player who is unable to draw a legal line loses.

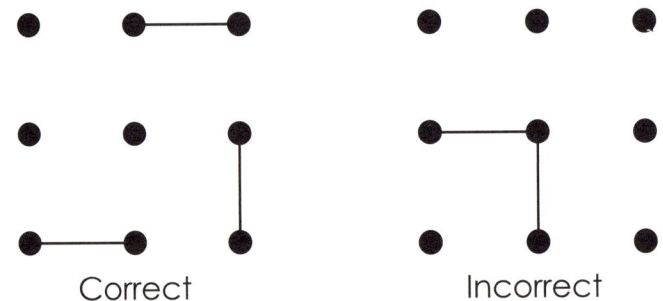

Correct   Incorrect

Explore 24: Shush-Hush Quiet Activities

Dynamic Dotted Duels

Ko No!

This is a two-person game. To play, you need a pencil and a piece of paper, as well as two playing pieces for each player. Playing pieces can be beans, candy, pebbles, etc. Draw a figure on the paper as shown below. One player places his two pieces on the top two dots. The other player places her pieces on the bottom two dots. The first player moves one piece to the middle. The other player moves a piece to the empty space. The object of the game is to block your opponent so that he or she cannot move. There is no jumping, and all moves must be made along the lines.

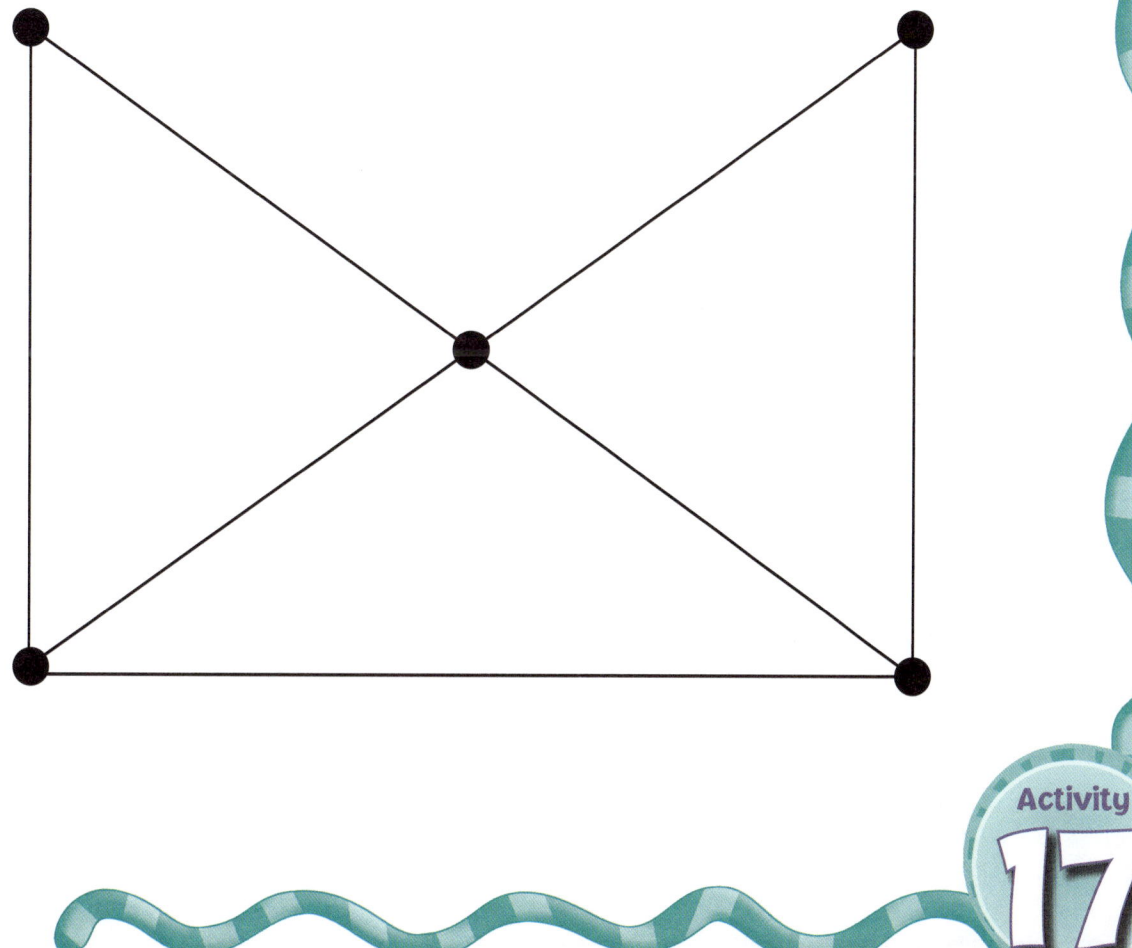

Activity 18

All in a Row?

Pretty maids all in a row? Ducks in a row? Row, row, row your boat? No need to cause a row; just put three in a row, and you win!

Tic-Tac-Toe

It's much easier to sit quietly when you have someone to pass the time with. Having fun games to play can help, too! Draw a grid as shown below. One player is X; the other is O. Players take turns marking an empty square. The first player to get three marks in a row is the winner. If all nine squares are full and no player has won, the game ends in a tie.

Explore 24: Shush-Hush Quiet Activities

All in a Row?

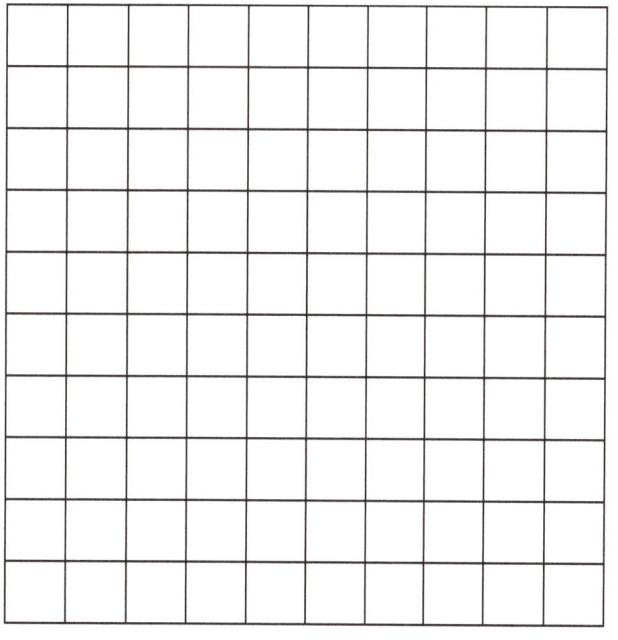

Five in a Row

Make a 10 x 10 grid on your paper. This game is a larger version of Tic-Tac-Toe. One player is X and the other is O. The object of this game is to be the first player to get five in a row.

Three in a Row

For this two-person game you will need four game pieces (two for each player), a piece of paper, and a pencil. The players' game pieces should be different. For example, one player might use two pennies and the other player two nickels. Draw a square with three lines dividing it as shown below. Take turns placing your pieces on the square. You may place pieces at the ends of any of the lines or in the center. Once all four pieces are on the board, take turns moving your pieces. The object is to get three pieces in a row. You can move pieces from one stopping point on a line to another. Jumping another piece is allowed. The first player to get three in a row—across, up and down, or diagonally—is the winner.

Activity 18

Toothpick Wonders

These games work best with toothpicks. But you can always just use pencil and paper if no toothpicks are around. You'll find all the solutions on page 48.

Add five toothpicks to these six toothpicks to make nine.

Use 12 toothpicks to make four squares as shown. The challenge: move three toothpicks to make three squares.

Use 24 toothpicks to make nine squares as shown. Now take away eight toothpicks, leaving two squares.

Arrange 13 toothpicks to make the dog as shown. The challenge: make the dog face the opposite direction by moving only two toothpicks.

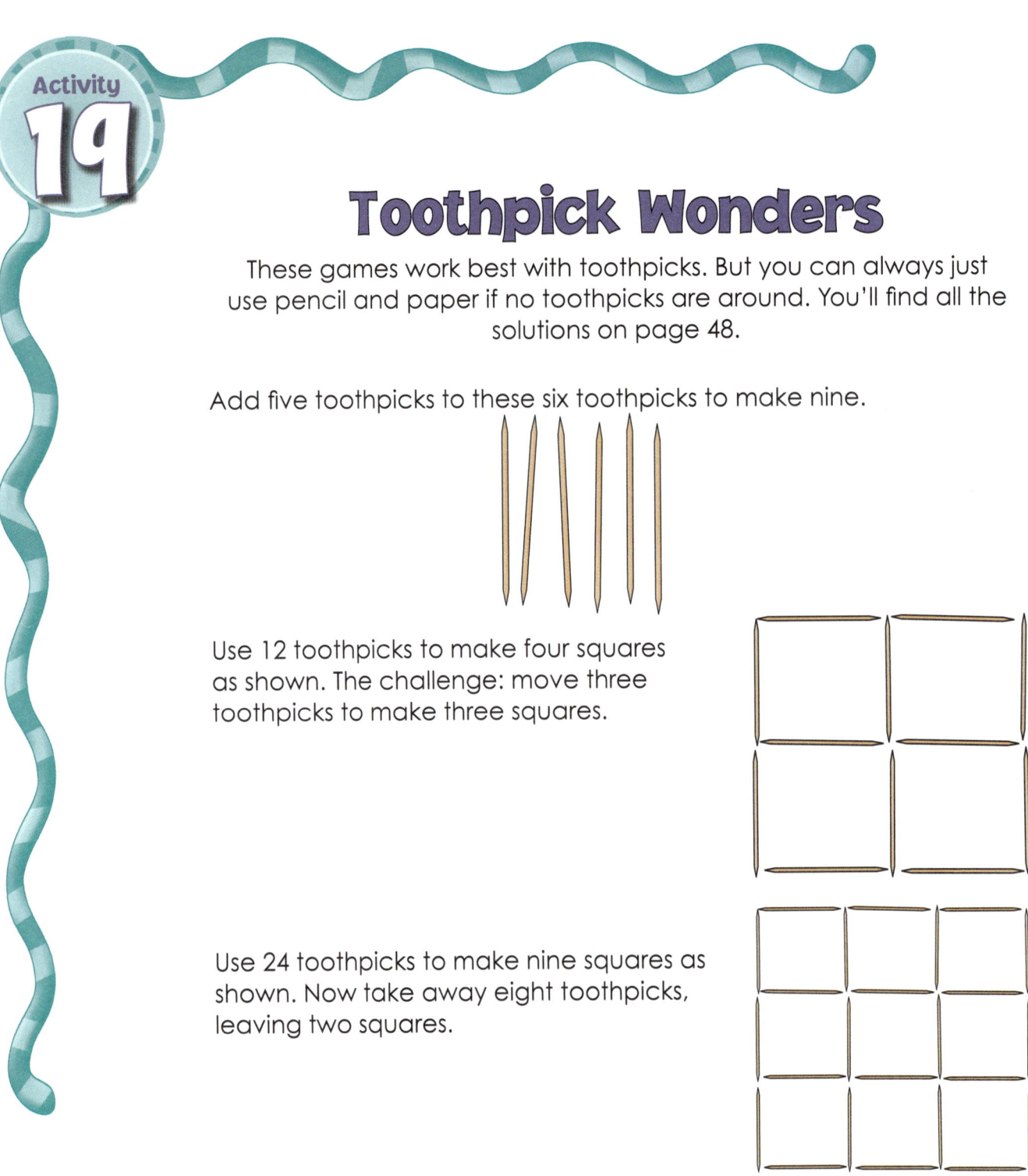

Toothpick Wonders

Nim

This ancient Chinese game is easy to play, but hard to win. You will need at least two players.

You'll need 16 toothpicks. Lay the toothpicks out flat. Each player, in turn, will take 1, 2, or 3 toothpicks at a time. The player to pick up the last stick loses.

For a twist, try this: Line up the 16 toothpicks in four columns. Players take turns taking 1, 2, 3, or 4 toothpicks from the same column or row. The toothpicks must be next to each other. The winner is the player that forces the other player to pick up the last toothpick.

Activity 20

Battle Brigade

Battle Brigade is similar to the game Battleship, only more portable. All you need is a pencil and some grid paper to play.

Make copies of page 35 or use a piece of grid paper and make a 10 x 10 grid. Label the grid as shown on page 35. Next, each player must secretly place his or her ships on the grid. Don't let the other player see your grid! Each player will mark five ships:

1 battleship—5 squares
1 cruiser—4 squares
2 destroyers—3 squares each
1 submarine—2 squares

Once both players are ready, the first player calls out a grid square (for example, J-2). If a boat is located in that square, the second player says, "Hit!" If there is no boat on the space, the player says, "Miss!" The players then switch roles, and the second player calls out a grid square. Once a player has hit all the squares of a ship, that ship has "sunk." Players must say when a ship has been sunk. The winner is the first person to sink all the opponent's ships.

Mark your charts using these symbols:
Mark the grid square with an X when you hit a ship. Mark the grid square with an M when you miss. Shade in the grid square when a part of your ship is hit. (You can put an O on the grid square when a shot misses your ships if you like.)

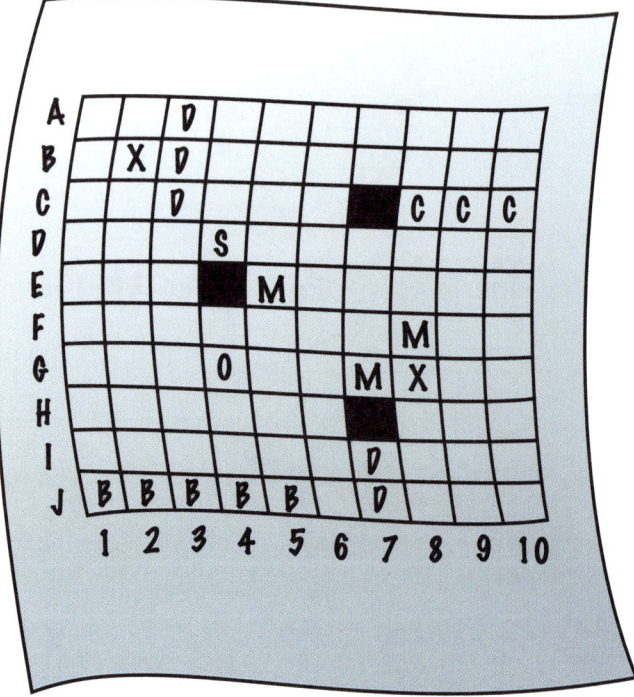

Explore 24: Shush-Hush Quiet Activities

Page 34

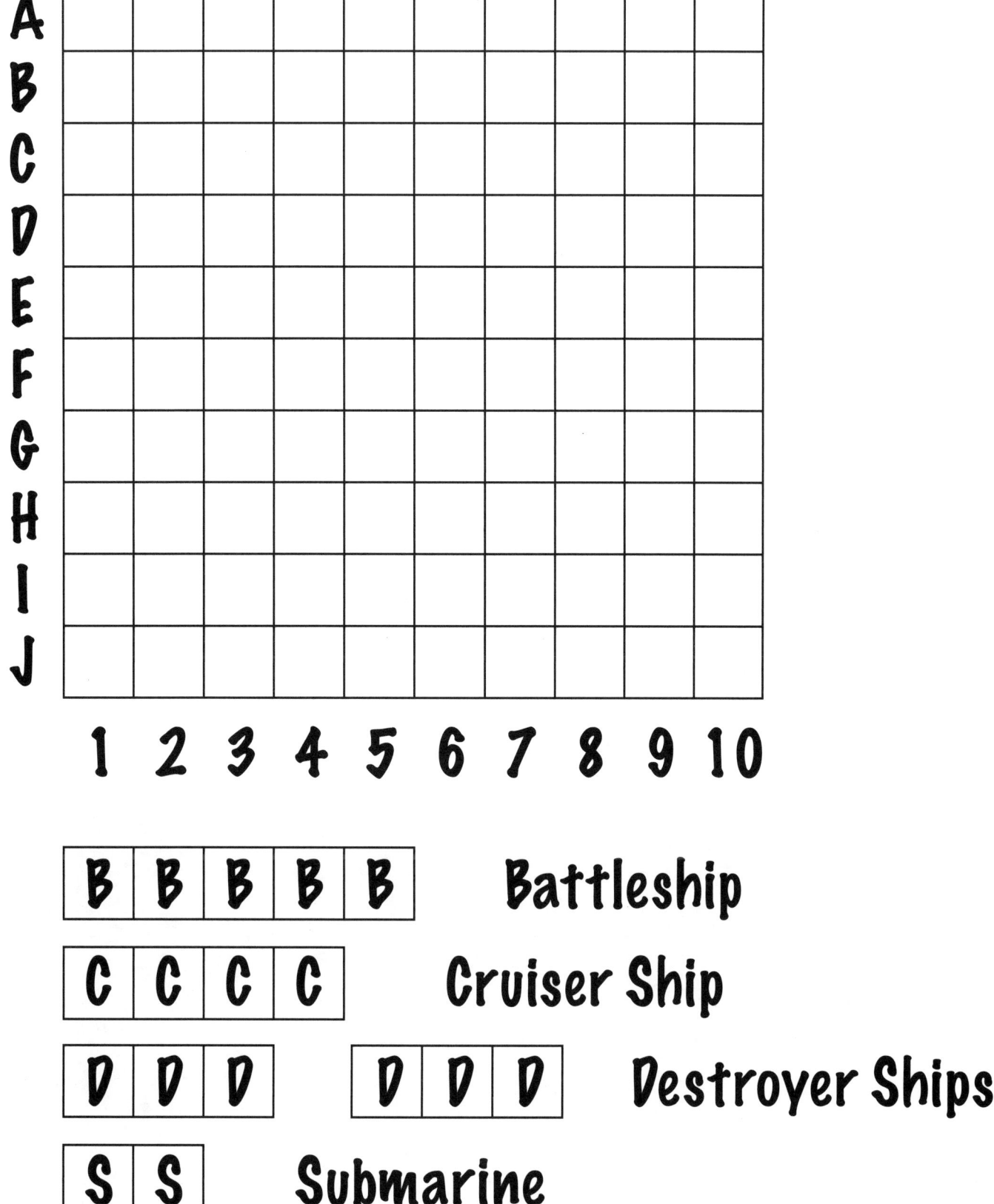

Activity 21

Penny for Your Thoughts

Next time your parents want you to be quiet, ask them for ten pennies. Then see if you can make "cents" of these penny games.

Traveling Triangle

Make a triangle using ten pennies as shown below. The challenge: reverse the triangle so that it points down instead of up by moving only three pennies. See page 48 for the solution.

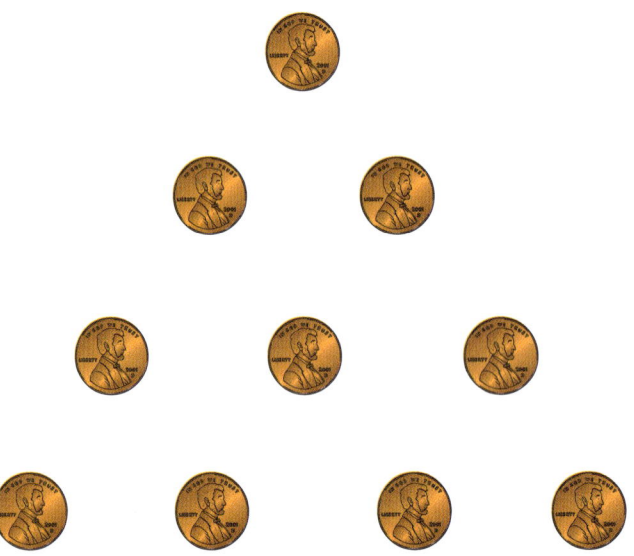

Catch the Coin

Balance a penny on your elbow. (Look at the picture to see how.) Then drop your hand and try to catch the penny before it hits the ground. For more of a challenge, try stacking two pennies on your elbow. See how many pennies you can stack and catch!

Explore 24: Shush-Hush Quiet Activities   Page 36

Explore 24: Shush-Hush Quiet Activities

Penny for Your Thoughts

Pennyball

Players sit on opposite sides of a table. The object of the game is to get the penny to hang over the edge without falling off the table. A player scores one point for doing this. Each player gets four tries. To move the coin, the players must flick it with their finger. If the player does not score in four turns it is the other player's turn.

If a player does score, he then tries to score an extra point. To do this, the other player makes a goal by putting the tips of her index fingers together with thumbs up. The player who scored the point then spins the coin and catches it with his thumbs. He then tries to toss the coin from between his thumbs through the goal posts. If the penny goes through the goal posts, he scores an extra point. If he fails, it's the other player's turn.

Not sure who should go first? Flip the coin and call it!

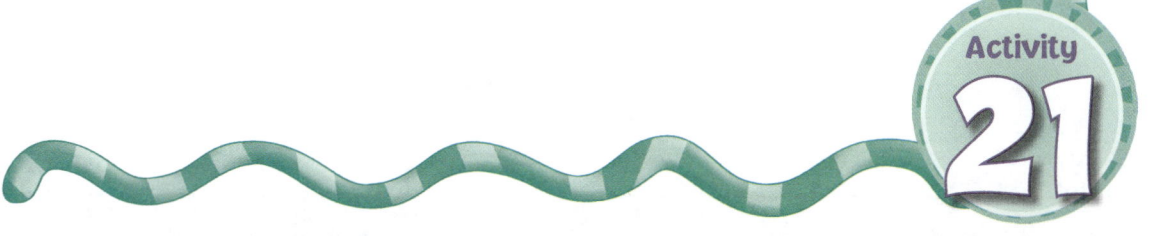

Activity 21

Activity 22

It's in the Cards

Need to stay quiet for a long time? Get a deck of cards.

Solitaire Match Up

First, you'll need to take all the cards less than seven out of your deck, except for the aces. Leave those in. Shuffle your new deck. Then place the cards into eight piles face up. There will be four cards in each pile. Remove any pairs from the top of the piles and set them aside. Continue to do this until you do not have any more pairs. To win the game, you must remove all the cards from the eight piles.

Explore 24: Shush-Hush Quiet Activities

Page 38

Explore 24: Shush-Hush Quiet Activities

It's in the Cards

Tell your mom not to worry; this war is just a game of cards.

War

This is a game for two players. Shuffle a deck of cards; then divide the deck in half. Each player gets half the deck. Players place their cards in a pile face down in front of them. The players turn the top card on their pile face up at the same time. The person with the highest card wins both cards. Aces are high in this game. If the players turn up cards with the same value, the war is on! Players place the next three cards from their pile face down in a pile and turn a fourth card up while stating, "I declare WAR!" Again, the person with the card with the highest value wins all the cards. If the cards are the same value again, another war occurs. The object of the game is to get all the cards.

Activity 22

Activity 22

Crazy Eights

Shuffle a deck of cards and deal seven cards to each player. Place the leftover cards face down in the middle. Turn the top card face up next to the pile.

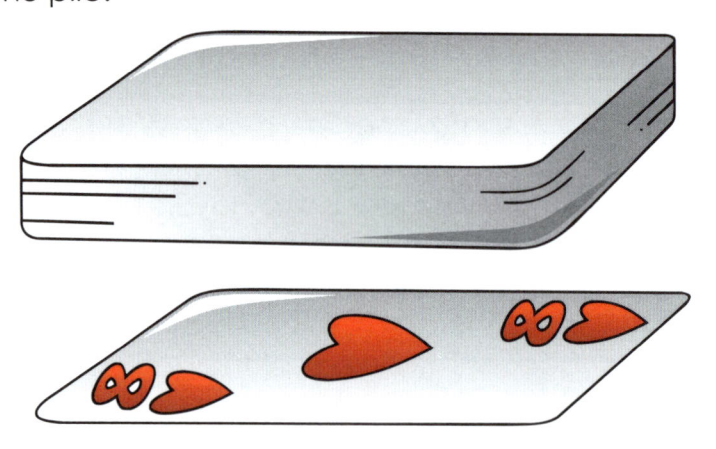

The first player plays a card on top of the card that is face up. To play a card it must be of the same suit (clubs, spades, diamonds, or hearts) or the same number. Eights are "wild" and can be played at any time. Whoever plays an eight calls out any suit they wish. If you have no cards that you can play, you must draw from the face-down pile until you pick up a card you can play. When the face-down pile runs out, turn the face-up cards over and shuffle them to make a new pile. The object of the game is to be the first player to play all your cards.

If an ace of hearts is up, you can...

play any heart   any ace   or any eight

Explore 24: Shush-Hush Quiet Activities

Page 40

Explore 24: Shush-Hush Quiet Activities

Page 41

Domino Delight

Dominoes

Cut out this domino set. You may want to tear this page out and glue it on a thin piece of cardboard before cutting out the individual pieces to make your dominoes sturdier. Store your set in an envelope. You will find rules on how to play on page 43.

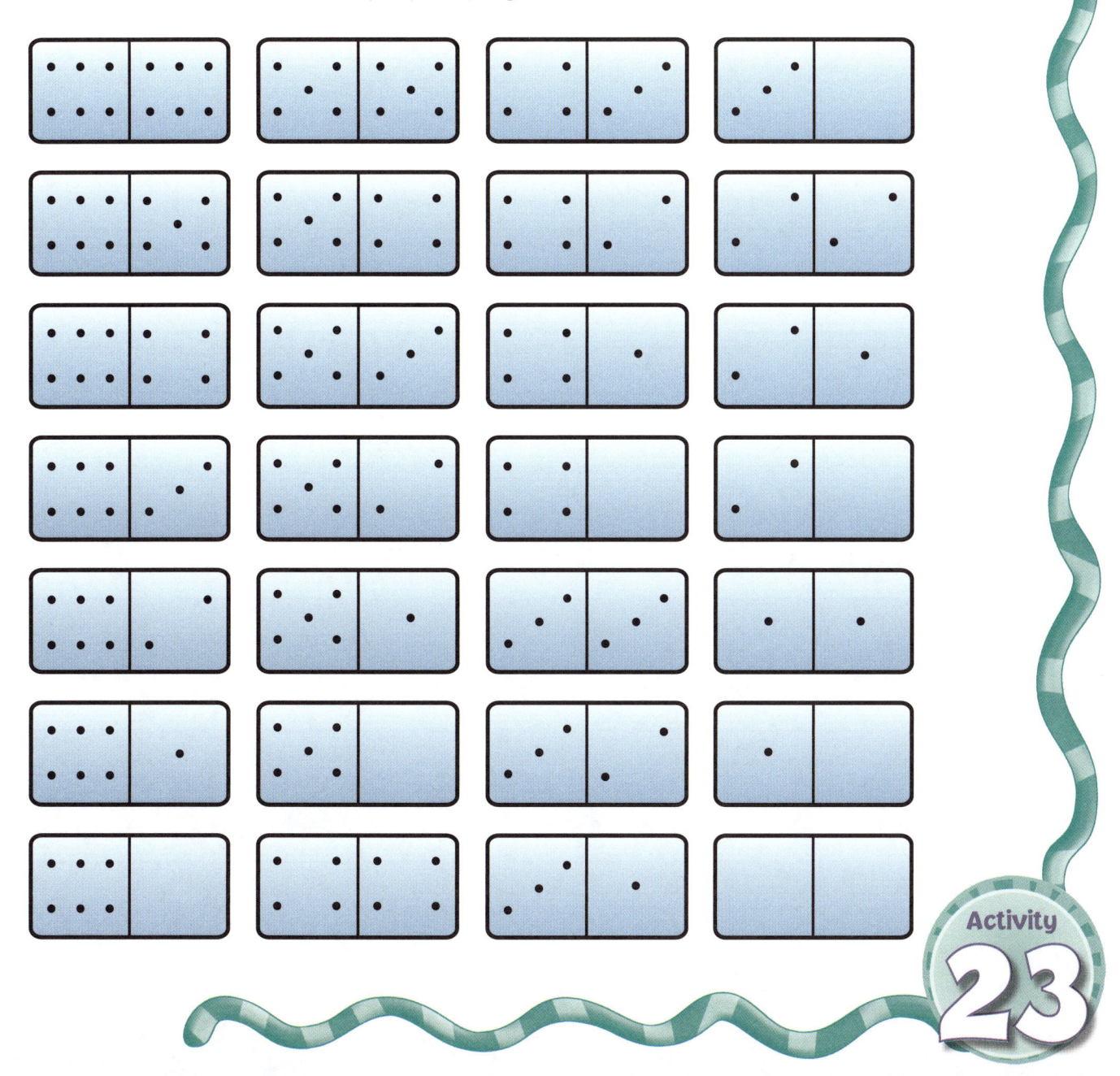

Activity 23

Domino Delight

How to Play Dominoes
To start, lay the dominoes with their dots down in the **boneyard**. (The boneyard is the pile of dominoes that haven't been drawn yet.) Each player draws seven dominoes. You may look at your own dominoes, but keep them so no one else can see the dots. The first player lays one domino face up. The next player has to play a domino that matches the dots on either of the ends. For example, if the first player puts down a domino with three dots on one end and five on the other, the second player could put down a domino that had either three or five dots on one end. If a player cannot play, she draws dominoes from the boneyard until she can play. The first player to play all her dominoes wins.

Solitaire Dominoes
Can't find anyone to play dominoes with? Just play by yourself. Place all the dominoes, dots down, in the boneyard. Draw seven dominoes. This time you may turn the dominoes up. Play your first domino. Then play as many of your dominoes as you can. When you cannot play or have used up all your dominoes, draw seven more dominoes from the boneyard. Continue until you have used all the dominoes or you can't play another piece.

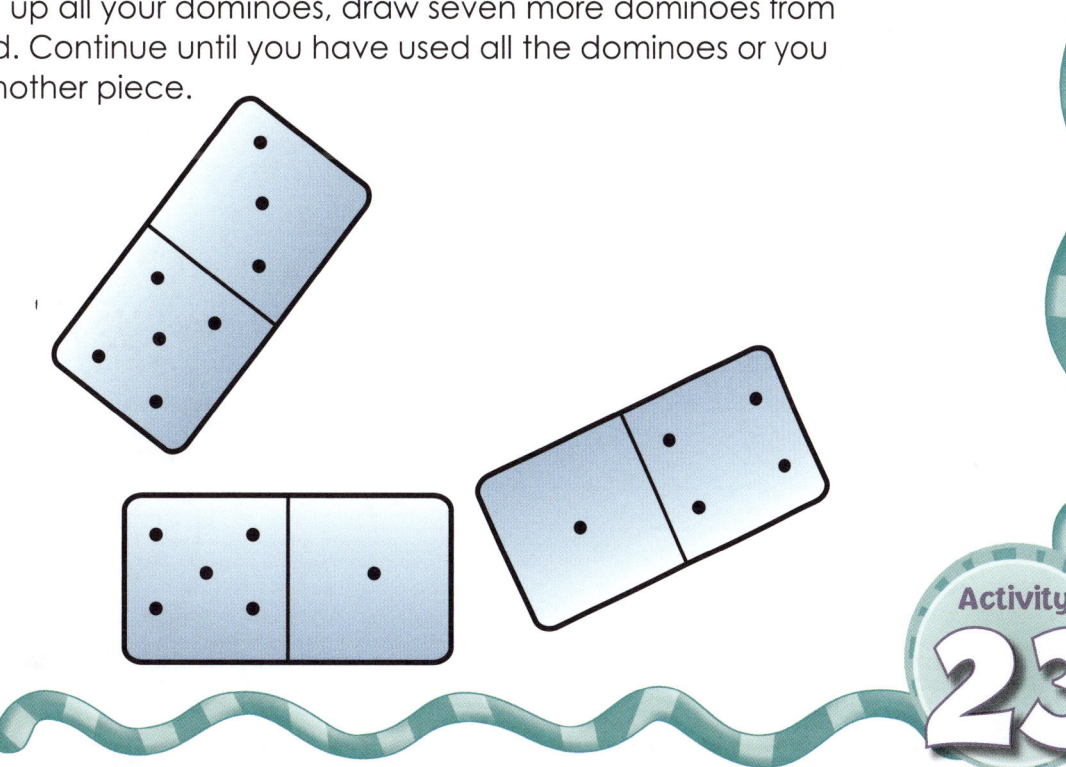

Activity 24

Tantalizing Tangrams

This ancient Chinese puzzle uses 7 simple pieces to make many different shapes and pictures. This puzzle has 5 triangles, 1 square, and 1 rhombus. Cut out the puzzle on page 45. Use the pieces to make some of the pictures below. Then create some of your own pictures and record them for others to solve.

Explore 24: Shush-Hush Quiet Activities

Page 44

Explore 24: Shush-Hush Quiet Activities   Page 45

Tantalizing Tangrams

Activity 24

Explore 24: Shush-Hush Quiet Activities

Solutions Page

Page 11

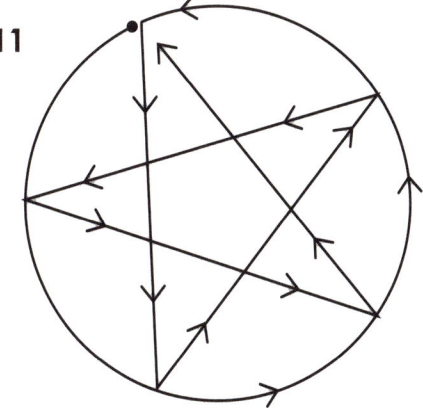

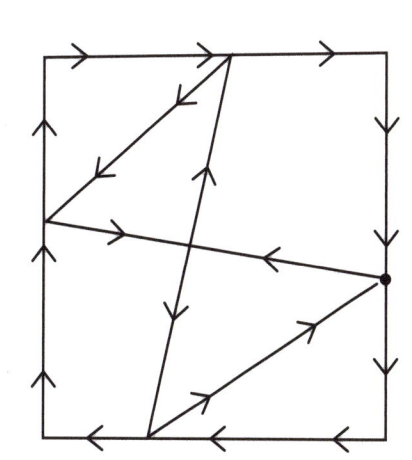

Page 14
Equal Numbers

9, 1, 2, 3
4, 5, 6
7, 8

It All Adds Up

5	0	3	12
5	0	9	6
8	7	4	1
2	13	4	1

Page 15
Silence is Golden

Page 24
Hush little baby.

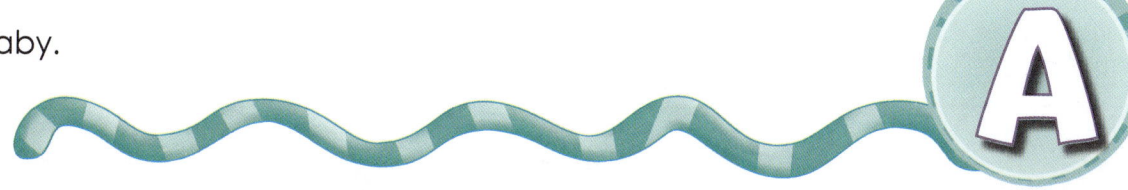

Solutions Page

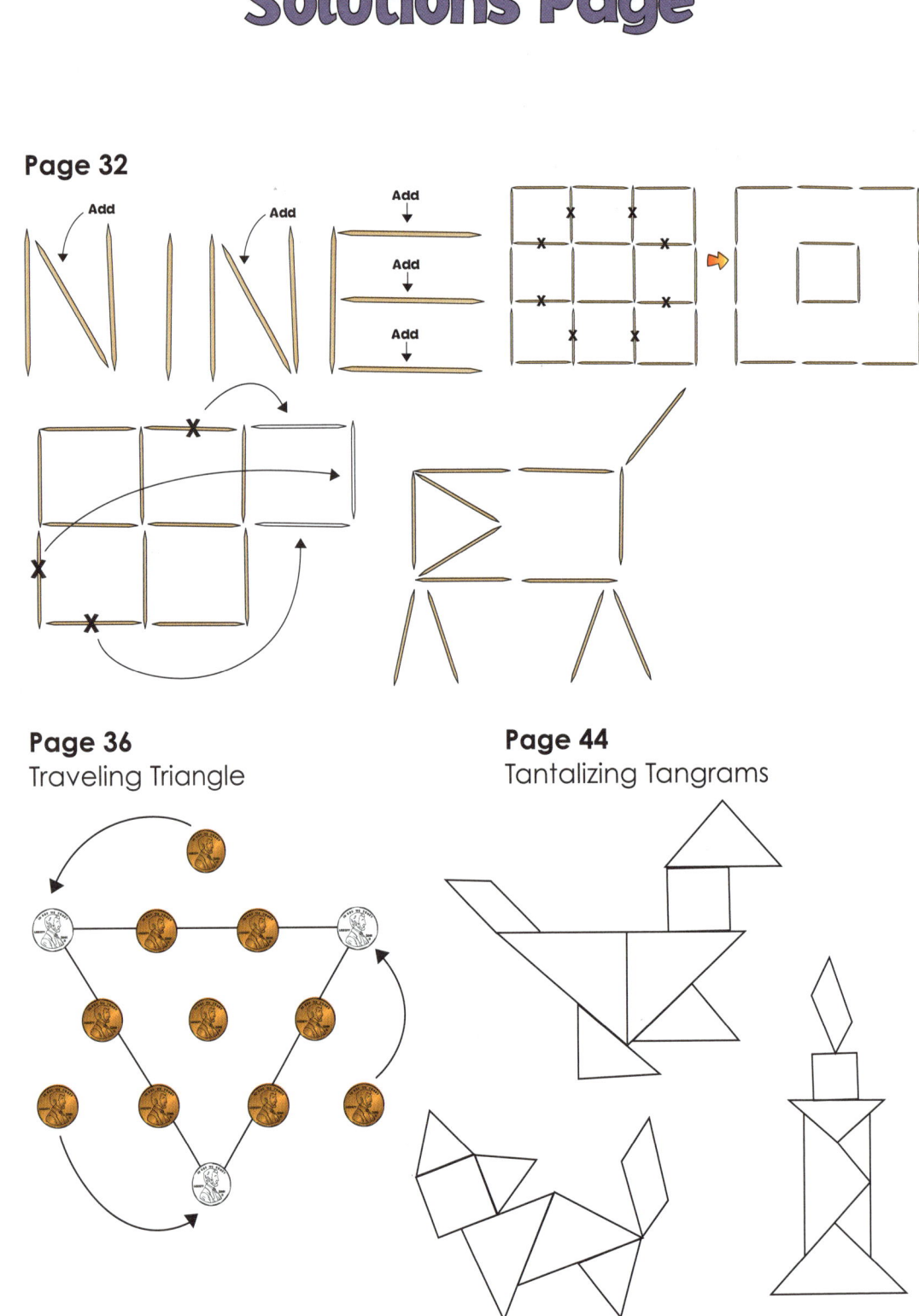

Page 32

Page 36
Traveling Triangle

Page 44
Tantalizing Tangrams

Explore 24: Shush-Hush Quiet Activities

Page 48